A Ba

Instruction

C000148830

A Baby's Little Instruction Book

David Brawn

HarperCollins*Publishers*

HarperCollins*Publishers*
77–85 Fulham Palace Road,
Hammersmith, London W6 8JB
www.fireandwater.com

First published by Thorsons 1995
Published by HarperCollins*Publishers* 2000

3 5 7 9 10 8 6 4 2

© David Brawn 1995

David Brawn asserts the moral right to be
identified as the author of this work

Illustrations by Mike Gordon

A catalogue record for this book
is available from the British Library

ISBN 0 00 710098 1

Printed and bound in Great Britain by
Martins the Printers Ltd, Berwick upon Tweed

To Sarah and Georgia
for such marvellous inspiration

And to their mummy, Tracey,
who did most of the research

Introduction

We all start our passage through life as babies. Like it or not, we've all been there, and when we come to have children ourselves, we encounter the same frustrations and make the same mistakes as all other parents, including our own. If a baby were writing his or her own manual, describing how best to embarrass or try the patience of the most switched-on parent, this is the book that would result. The 300 or so instructions are just a few of the inevitable infuriations babies cause as they learn the boundaries of social behaviour and push their parents near the ends of tethers they had no idea could be so long. The book *may* serve as preparation for the unsuspecting new parent, but is probably no more practical than any affectionate tribute to the ingenuity and inventiveness of those who shall inherit our future. Thank goodness they all – eventually – grow up!

And just what *is* a baby? As far as *A Baby's Little Instruction Book* goes, if it covered only the first six months of life, it would likely contain just four instructions, detailing the processes of sleeping, crying, eating and filling one's nappy (or diaper, if you prefer). I have therefore chosen to include the early toddling years, up to about three and a half, when most children are canny enough to have become mini-adults in their own right – they certainly expect to be treated as such. The instructions themselves are not arranged in any particular order – babies develop at different rates, and some will talk before they can walk, cut their first teeth before they sleep through the night, or embark on potty training before they draw on the wallpaper. To try to impose a progressive order in the book would therefore be quite impossible. Suffice it to say, for those readers with babies and young children of their own, if you are not yet familiar with any of the items of behaviour mentioned, rest assured your little cherub will be doing these very soon!

Give Teddy open heart surgery

Insist on being breastfed until after you've cut your first teeth

Drink from fish bowls

Wipe sticky hands on a visitor's dress

Demolish shop window displays

If you find a tiny hole in a jumper, pull at it until it's no longer a tiny hole

Don't waste a good drink – only ever spill one if you know it will stain

Demand to watch the same video over and over and over again

Scream in the supermarket

Always embarrass an older brother or sister among schoolfriends

Call the childminder 'Mummy' in front of your own mother

Always find an excuse not to go clothes shopping

Use the toilet on display in a DIY store

Remember that 'Don't touch' is a licence to handle things

Suckle on anything vaguely nipple-shaped

Sneeze without due care and attention

Suck the label

Insist on your own ice cream cone – not just a lick of someone else's

Refuse to eat your dinner, yet have room for dessert

Develop a special cry for real emergencies

Carry a newborn brother or sister when no one is looking

Develop rashes that look far worse than they are

Never believe an adult who tells you a plate, teapot or radiator is hot – insist on investigating for yourself, then crying as though it's *their* fault

Learn to open child safety locks

- Jam your baby walker behind the door

- Leave sticky handprints on photographs

- Dribble in other people's drinks

- Block the toilet with laundry

Prefer a cassette to mummy
reading a story

Turn off the television when
they're watching the news

Push the stop button on
escalators

Learn to tell realistic tales

Be an angel at the childminder's and a monster at home

Embarrass your parents at every opportunity

🍼 Don't let Mummy use you as an excuse to queue-jump at the Ladies

🍼 Experiment with your mother's make-up bag

🍼 Change the rules to suit yourself

Jump on the bed

Burst your balloon and then believe the world has come to an end

Only choose breakfast cereal by virtue of the free gift

Do not allow your pram to be used as a substitute shopping trolley

Refuse to take your medicine

Be able to identify medicine even if 'disguised' in food or drink

Throw toys out of your pram and have people go back to look for them

Impress Granny with your new tricks

Never go out without your comforter

- Never allow your dirtiest soft toy to be washed

- Crayon in story books

- Go organic – eat mud

- Start a collection of sharp objects

Play with peas on your plate – don't under any circumstance *eat* them

Stick marbles up your nose

Tear covers off magazines

Play with wrapping paper and ignore the presents

Ask for your potty *after* the event

Invent new names for things and insist on using them until the whole family is doing it

Learn to feign injury

Pull at loose joins in the wallpaper

Never be seen in clothes handed down from a child of the opposite sex

Don't speak if pointing will do

Learn to distinguish between the sexes

Pick up bad language from your parents quicker than any other words

If you're going to lie, do it convincingly

Hate having your hair washed

Tell people you're an orphan for sympathy

Blow bubbles – eat soap

Only poo in the bath if you're sharing it with a parent

Throw up in the car without giving warning

Be unable to blow your nose properly

Have your parents take you out for a walk in the night to get you back to sleep

Call your maternal grandmother to her face by the name your father uses when she's not there

Pick your nose

Empty waste paper bins

Don't let your mother raid your money box to pay the milkman

Don't admit to missing your parents when they leave you at a relative's for the night

Insist on junk food in preference to healthy alternatives

Prove that no nappy is leak-proof

Never take 'No' for an answer

Always wipe your mouth after
being kissed by an elderly relative

Train your parents, but let them
think they're training you

Don't sit still when having your
hair cut

- Fall out of bed without waking up

- Be reluctant to share your toys with other children

- Enjoy repetitive musical toys that grate on adults' nerves

Be afraid of Father Christmas

Talk all the way through your first visit to the cinema

Don't let the arrival of another baby in the household lead to you being ignored

Induce heart attacks – stand up in your high-chair

When learning to stand up, ensure you know how to sit down again

Perfect the art of moving around only when you're on your own

Sleep in the same bed as your parents when:
a) You have nightmares
b) You're poorly
c) You know they want to try and expand the family!

Be ticklish

Refuse to eat the meals that have taken the longest to prepare

Ensure your first ever homemade Christmas decorations are displayed prominently, no matter how amateurish they look

Be ashamed of your parents

Don't eat chips without ketchup

Don't eat anything without chips

Fill your nappy immediately it's been changed

Sneeze with your mouth full

Poke at people's eyes

Ensure your parents never have the time to get up to anything

Demand attention during *Coronation Street*

❀ Never be tempted to pull at fake jewellery – only the real thing

❀ Suck your thumb

❀ Play with coal

Insist on being rocked to sleep, no matter how long it takes

Ensure more dinner goes in your hair than your mouth

Burst other toddlers' balloons

Say 'What?'

Show your underwear to strangers

Be able to retrieve a small morsel of vegetable out of a mouthful of food

Suck your top lip until your nose stops running

Learn to say 'No' before you learn to say 'Yes'

Insist on having as many lights on as possible at night

Fall asleep in Mummy's bed, but threaten to wake up when being transferred back to your cot, so you can stay in the warm

Wear your shoes on the wrong feet

Exhibit irrational terror at the sight of a uniform

No matter how long it takes, never stop crying until they give in

Wee in the swimming pool

Don't drink the water in the swimming pool

Stare at people in the changing room

Attempt to breastfeed from anybody who picks you up

Get your legs stuck between the bars of your cot

Say 'please' – it is the quickest route to getting your own way

Fake serious illness, and recover in the time it takes to get to the doctor's

Throw up on clean clothes

Lose your bootees when you're out

Put sweets in the shopping trolley which won't be noticed until after they've been paid for

Never be seen in a frilly sunhat

Eat out of your bib in preference to your bowl

Be adventurous with your food – worms, woodlice, snails, but *never* greens

Answer the telephone before anyone can get to it

Wriggle fiercely when having your nappy put on

When being changed, stick your feet in the dirty nappy before it's been taken off the changing mat

Develop a squint

Never stay pristine for very long

Avoid having a dirty face 'cleaned' with a grown up's tissue covered in spit!

Climb on the furniture, especially at other people's houses

Press your face up against shop windows

Leave handprints on mirrors

Eat off other people's plates, but not your own

Have a favourite plaything that isn't a toy

Remember, if God had intended you to use cutlery, he'd have given you metal fingers

Drop your dummy in the font at your Christening

Play with fragile ornaments

Talk to strangers

 Don't let bribery lead you to give up something you really want

 Learn how to play one parent off against the other

Be selectively deaf when being called

Demand that baby wipes are warmed before application

Never keep a secret

Open other people's presents

Insist on an expensive novelty toothbrush

Hide the television remote controller

Pull the tape out of cassettes

Don't drink from a cup in place of a bottle

 Tell your grandparents they're wrinkly

 Pull off toupées

 Skid around on your potty

- Empty visitors' handbags

- Demand coins from strangers

- Jump in puddles in unsuitable footwear

- Eat play dough

Never walk when you can ride in the pushchair

Eat out of the cat's dish

Learn how to 'accidentally' telephone the emergency services

Pull heads off flowers

Get plenty of sleep during the day
so you are at your wakeful best
throughout the night

Have temper tantrums over trivial
matters in very public places

Pull the cat's tail

Bite hard when someone's feeling your new teeth

Don't trust a man with a beard

In a room full of people, always make a beeline for the one who hates children

Always wee during a nappy change

Give the dog a haircut

Manage to reach things even when they're supposed to be out of reach

Don't let your parents get away with imposing a sweetie-free diet

Never take the blame for anything

- Pull ugly faces when being photographed for a cute baby competition

- Never show any intelligence during formal assessments

- Make rude noises from every orifice, and smile

If you build a snowman, don't plan a long-term relationship with him

Don't be afraid to learn traditional rhymes, and boycott any 'politically correct' versions

Play with toys that promote sexual stereotypes – of the opposite persuasion!

Walk in the gutter

If you go anywhere particularly 'grown up', endeavour to be especially naughty

Insist on 'having a word' on every telephone conversation

Ask your parents what sex is at an unreasonably young age – they won't be expecting the question

Talk with your mouth full

Have a box of tissues ready for the ritual kissing goodbye

Crayon on the wallpaper in preference to writing paper

Tell tales

Be friendly towards total strangers yet scream hysterically at close relatives

Lock yourself inside the car with the keys

 When potty training:
a) Remember to pull your pants down
b) Display your achievements to all and sundry
c) Don't wee over the edge

Don't have such a silly name for your private parts that people don't know what you're telling them about

When sleeping in Mummy's bedroom, snuffle and wheeze so she can't sleep

Dance to *Top of the Pops*

Never call the milkman 'Dad' (unless he is)

Know where the biscuits are kept and when they have not, in fact 'all gone'

Learn to count from 1 to 10, but not necessarily in that order

- Say 'Sorry' when you've been naughty (even if you're not)

- Pester to be taken out to play when Mummy's got a hangover

- Always discover contraceptives, no matter how well hidden, and ask what they are

Show your inquisitiveness by taking your auntie something she's really afraid of, like a mouse

Scream at your Christening, even before you get to the bit with the water

Expect to be fed on demand – just like Daddy

Instil a sense of parental guilt by yelling at your inoculations, even if you can't feel a thing

Get your fingers caught in the holes in your blanket

Learn to pull out electrical socket covers

When putting trousers on, only lift your left foot *after* you've put your right foot back on the floor – or you'll fall over

Blaspheme, just as Daddy does, at Playgroup

Disfigure your favourite teddy bear with too much love